Tangles

Holly Schindler

Tangles

Hardcover Edition Published by InToto Books

Copyright © 2018 by Holly Schindler

Cover and interior design by Holly Schindler

Cover image by newyear, courtesy of Shutterstock
Spring Market - Rustic Font by Beck McCormick and Saltery Brush Font by Pana Type & Studio, both courtesy of Creative Market
Swirls Swirls Swirls Photoshop Brush by Louise Wagstaff/DigiTreats and Scattered Confetti Photoshop Brush by Jessie Hutchison/jhCollaborative, both courtesy of Etsy

Table of Contents

Tangles

Tangles

it's what happens

to your

heart

your

thoughts

the you and me

the now and then

the way it was

and the way I

wish it was

the love and the

battles

the goosebumps

and silence

the distance

and embraces

the truth

and the

Tangles

half-truths

and the

outright

lies

even

lies told

to make things

prettier

all the knots

all tangled up

in the sweetness

and the sorrow

and the dreaming

and the remembering

Tangles

From Strawberries to Gin

From Strawberries to Gin

Even at that silly ice cream parlor
we were separated,
each of us on either side of the
marble table,
my girly, frothy pink soda
and your unfussy single scoop
blocking our view of one another.

But something more
stood between us:
your pierced ears and sideburns,
my naked face and boyish hips...

You leaning into the corner of the booth,
foot in the seat, arm draped across your knee
while I jiggled a skinny leg and picked at cuticles,
picturing the drive beneath your sunroof and our
        curbside arrival:

My anxious reflection in the window,
your breath on my cheek,
how I should tilt my head, close my eyes——
so much to consider beneath street lamps.

but automatic for you.
Awkward. fumbling. I tried to tell myself then
I would master the task
of becoming a grown-up. As suspected.

I have since learned how to wear red lipstick
and order a martini...How to make use of my mouth
and to swallow my fears
by adopting the collected pose of you.

From Strawberries to Gin

Static

you flick on the radio

and it sounds like

your doubts

like you don't think

we're managing

to live up to

what's playing

in your mind

all those castles of

perfection

and a summer

picnic blanket

you twist and twist

and you can't

seem to find

what it is
that you're looking for

the right sound
the right rhythm
the perfect melody

and that's just
how it goes
a minor chord
gives a pop song
better texture

if it rains
we will laugh
it will make
the picnic
more
memorable
don't you know
it's the dreams
that are crooked
that make better stories

so it's fine

Static

it's okay
it never has
to be perfect

whatever you dial in

sometimes, it's static
sometimes, it's song

This Is Not a Song About a Man

This Is Not a Song About a Man

She learned to play guitar
in the era
of cassette tapes and
garage bands,
sitting on an
overturned milk crate, her fingers
yellowing with new calluses,
knees jutting from the jaws of
stonewashed denim rips.

She cut her nails
for more control over the strings.
She swore she'd given up on hair dye, too,
and tight skirts and trying too hard.

This Is Not a Song About a Man

She would play
like all the men——
loud and distorted and
unapologetic.

Her teacher was
in a band, rented studio
space to practice, and sold his own
self-produced albums.
He taught her to chord and
kiss
without second-thought.

She learned the rest
from music magazines with tab.

This Is Not a Song About a Man

Blushing

Crimson

Blushing Crimson

summer heat

riverbank

bare feet

heart harpooned

so complete

beers we drank

whispers sweet

breeze in June

faces meet

giggles clank

kisses heat

clothing strewn

emotions piqued

bodies sank

love discreet

under a blushing crimson moon

Ancient

History

Ancient History

My last boyfriend
was a tattoo artist,
she explained,
half-smile,
of the reptile
coiling
between her
shoulder blades.

When he tried
to hide the ink,
draping his
jacket
across her
back,
she said,
The only difference
is that she left her mark
inside you.

Tell

the Night I

Tell the Night 1

You can tell the night
I'm leaving,
I'll board the first
star ship that comes.

I'll slough off any
darkness,
shed it like a skin.
I won't succumb.

Tell heartbreak
it can dance
with the constellations
up above,

and since I'm still not
too strong to miss him,
tell the night
I send my love.

Summer

Is. . .

Summer Is...

the drop of sweat
trickling down the side
of the glass at the
bar
that evaporates
while the crowd is watching the band.

You are...
a page I'd written on somewhere,
wadded, then smoothed out again
over a desktop.

I'd had to change my mind about you,
as easy an offering as a blues riff
floating through the night air
into my ear
without even having to
ask.

Summer Is...

Easy as a man who bellows. "Come inside."
and collects the cover charge,
his wrists thick enough
to instantly hide what I've handed over,
like there's never been a price to pay
at all.

Hard to believe in easiness, though.

I had to refuse you then,
create a space between,
a polite distance in a front seat,
so that later on,
on a long July drive
I'd rub my elbow on the armrest
and reveal
the raw spot I'd created by
trying
to lean in closer
to you.

Summer Is...

Sunday Morning

Sunday Morning

Woke up with the sunlight
tangled round my legs.
Woke up with a rainbow
in my head.

Woke up to a rhyme
barking at me, begging.
Woke up to words
still left unsaid.

Woke up to a secret:
I wiped the cobwebs
from my heart.
I no longer see
your eyes among the stars.

Sunday Morning

Once you were the moon
that kept my world bright
through the night.
and I was the sun who rose
just to chase you across the sky.

No longer waiting
for you to cross
the doorstep of my
heart.
I've stopped
loving you
from afar.

Sunday Morning

Things
I Have
Stolen

Things I Have Stolen

So many worthless
trinkets:
Plastic barrettes, hotel towels,
a Buddy Holly flea market pin.

More important
baubles:
A heart, a man——
at least,
before she stole him back.

You are not shiny, either.
Your mouth is like a restaurant fork
handled by so many girls before me.
You've been stolen
a time or two.
We're looking used up to each other.

Things I Have Stolen

This damn diner's as common as this love.
Our waitress has seen an unending stream
of you's and me's.
In a few weeks,
when I stop running
from this awful ending, I'll think of it: The forgotten tip,
no longer spare change and cheap as a shrug.
It will weigh on me,
like robbery.

Things I Have Stolen

Human

After

All

Human After All

Can you listen to the gears inside me
start to turn?
Do you believe in the
mechanics
of forgiveness?

Paperback perfection——
romance novels
swear it still
exists.

But Friday nights were never
any sacrifice
spent wondering who caught you
from your fall.
And it never crossed my mind
that I should
think it over twice.

so maybe I am not so
human
after all.

Nine O'Clock and Our Conversation Has Spun Itself Out

Firemen

across the street

engage in three-on-three,

wet rings

appearing under

shirt-sleeves.

sneakered feet

rising above the

pavement

as the ball

rolls

from fingertips and

taps

the crooked backboard

the orange rim.

You stand

ankle deep

Nine O'Clock and Our Conversation...

in front yard
grass.
consuming
your cigarette.
sending out
round, orange
flares
with the rest
of the lightning bugs.

My sandals
clomp
against your hardwood
floors.
Sweet summer quiet night,
you can hear me.
You can see me, too,
on the other side of the
screen door silver grid.
I have combed my hair,
reapplied my lipstick.

It is time to go.

Behind your shoulder

Nine O'Clock and Our Conversation...

under the night sky,
the yellow-apple engine
sits in the blackened
firehouse,
as grown men continue to
spit, slap hands,
shout adolescent threats,
bump shoulders into chests,
and argue over boundary lines...

as though they, too,
know there will be no fire tonight.

Fortune Cookie

Fortune Cookie

Winter dawns
gray November.
Drizzle drips from the
awnings of buildings
like tears
from eyelash
fringe.

The pupil of a front window——
mostly black. except for
the reflection of
you and me
curled and swirled
into each other

Fortune Cookie

on the same

side

of a red vinyl booth,

our words

tangling

and

twisting

around

one another.

Like a wishbone,

we crack

our future's container,

exposing only a

blank

white strip of paper.

You refuse

to believe it,

and sift through

broken

bits of pastry,

convinced of finding

something more.

Fortune Cookie

Tenderness Mining

Tenderness Mining

You have to dig deep
to get the
good stuff
the real stuff

It's not something
you fake
or imitate
or play

It's not an act
or a white lie
or a slant of truth

It's not a promise
you make
so that you
can take
and escape.

You have to dig deep
to get
to the
good stuff.

The
Idea
of
You

The Idea of You

I could lie to you
and tell you I don't miss you anymore.
Or I could lie to you
and tell you that I do.

I could call you up
just to tell you that I'm sorry.
Or I could call you up
just to remind you that I'm not.

But I think I'm just going to sit here
and miss the idea of you.

You're far from perfect.
You're no courageous hero——
(You know the kind.
all muscle-bound and usually
starring in one of those
action flicks
or if you want to get

The Idea of You

old-fashioned
and borderline
cliché
about it. maybe one of
those cowboy types
on a stallion.)

But now you're gone,
and I can turn you into
whatever I want
in my mind.
Now you're gone,
and I think I like
sitting here
being
tragic.

The Idea of You

Golden
Lasso

Golden Lasso

She was married
to the bartender
by then,
by the time
the fantasies
started.
She knew it was a
silly thing
to lean on them,
the same way
she knew the man who should've
loved her didn't. Still,
she served
the construction workers,
the ones who stopped
at the door to kick
mud from their steel-toed
boots. They knew

all the right jokes, and she
sometimes gave free beers for the
dirtiest ones. Her husband
got a TV, bought it at a
yard sale so
the workers could watch
the car races and rodeos. He moved
like a man without purpose
behind the counter, like
a story already told.
And she was dreaming about
the construction worker
who reminded her of Elvis,
and a wedding band left behind
once in an ashtray. She and her
husband turned the
cash register
into a lost and found,
kept the ring under the drawer.
She tried the band on
when he wasn't looking, pretended
it wasn't too big for her
thumb. Imagined it and
the sound of popping gravel
outside were hers.

Golden Lasso

This
Secret

This Secret

There's no honor
in a back door.

but then again,
I have
no impressive
pedigree.

this secret is safe with me

Tiptoeing feels a little
sneaky——

but then again,
it's got
a tone of
intrigue

This Secret

this secret is safe with me

There's nothing wrong
with kissing right out
in the
sunlight.

but then again,
I know you'd never
agree——

you went and fell
for someone
not in your league

this secret
is safe
with
me.

This Secret

Tonight, It's All Right

Tonight, It's All Right

The way you've been
leaning
on doorways
tells me
you've got escape
on your mind.

You're dreaming of lips
you haven't yet kissed
a world full of arms that aren't mine.

It's all right if your hand's on the doorknob
it's all right if you're dreaming of
wild things
and lightning

Tonight, It's All Right

that never
strikes twice.

It's all right if you're dreaming of weather
and shucking the safety of
shelter

It's all right if you're already leaving
it's all right if you're taking to
flight

something tells me
that your heart is already
the coldest
of lonely
midnights

but once we believed
our days
would all swelter——

and once,
the wild thing
you ran to
was me.

Tonight, It's All Right

Maybe words have a way of
pretending
or trying to
apply a
sugarcoat

Maybe you've already
decided
to sow a whole field of
wild oats...

but tonight.
(one more night)
it's all right if you don't.

Things We Do for Luck

Things We Do for Luck

Rub a stone

pluck a clover

carry a trinket.

avoid ladders and mirrors

——don't even think it——

all to

turn an eye

get a wink

get a second look

get a question

get attention

get a hint of affection

get somebody hooked

and though you might dream it

——you wouldn't dare scream it——

Things We Do for Luck

(or murmur

or whisper

for fear you were

about to become

a great saboteur)

the luckiest thing

in the world

is to feel

free enough

to risk

using the

word

love.

Things We Do for Luck

Kaleidoscope

Kaleidoscope

It's more than
one mirror
it's a double
reflection

like two pairs of
eyes
looking
back at each other
turning
nothing more
than bits of
broken beads
or shards
or fragments
into a
single
piece of
connected
unified
beauty.

Approaching

Autumn

Approaching Autumn

I wonder

if summer romances

hover in the

background

of the

love stories

that begin

in the autumn of

life.

Maybe they are

hotter

Approaching Autumn

twice as hot
as the first time
around

and maybe all the
hearts
singe the very
air
they touch

and maybe
it's hearts
starting over
that turn
the leaves
the color
of fire.

Approaching Autumn

Fast as I Can Fall

Fast as I Can Fall

Morning sky is glowing,
birds are softly crowing,
dew-drenched grass is flowing
like a melody.

Another day is dawning,
in a blink the stars come calling.
But that's nothing——
you should see
how fast my heart can fall.

No more winter glooming
with morning glories blooming.
Buds and babies and the green upon the vine.

Fast as I Can Fall

Nothing takes root quicker
than when love begins to flicker.
There is nothing
quite as fast as I can fall.

Do we ache to love
at full speed?
No warnings ever to heed?
Do we want to lay
our hearts
right on the
line?

For a love as soft as a breeze,
with a power that rocks me
to my knees

I'll come running——
just as fast
as I can
fall.

Fast as I Can Fall

A View

from

Inside Out

A View from Inside Out

The youngest daughter stands on the front porch,
calves flexed by five-inch heels, straps spelling
offers of love: "Xs" across the toes,
"O"s around the ankles.

Inside, the oldest women in the family
sit at the kitchen table
all of them relics,
widows.
Girls treat the older generations
like knickknacks.

They know.
They have stood where she stands.

It is, they insist, always
the same story.

dressed in different fashion.

But the girl on the porch
is too young
to know anything but the same
Not me
the widows declared decades ago.

Heartbreak, she has decided,
is old-fashioned.

She is immune.
Maybe she will be.
But the widows believe
differently.

They shake their heads,
making their white hair
ripple as they
stare through the window
and watch
the same
(yes, yes the same)
story begin
all over again——

A View from Inside Out

a girl waiting

for her date's car

to roll into the driveway

before she

dares to venture past the front step.

Fade

Fade

Back then,

it felt like everything was blooming.

Mostly, me.

(Memory,

come take your bow.)

Back then,

you floated through my mind.

Mostly, without warning.

(Memory,

come take your bow.)

Back then,

I had you memorized

romanticized

dramatized

eroticized

eternalized

Fade

I empathized

and have since
realized
I fictionalized
rationalized
demonized
despised

till your
baby blue eyes
grew hazier
like all things
idealized——

until they were

impossible

to
remember
at all.

(Memory.
come take your bow.)

Fade

Raspberry Regrets

Raspberry Regrets

You carry them always
sour-sweet
what-ifs
almost-was-es
could-have-beens
what-abouts

Occasionally,
they overpower——
like the clank of
traffic
that drowns out the
radio
on the first
spring day

Raspberry Regrets

warm enough
to roll the windows down.

But the sun, the
wind
on your stale
seasoned skin
lets you know
that's a cross
you can easily
bear.

Raspberry Regrets

Untangled

Untangled

and sometimes

it is clear

it is simple

it's not complicated

at all

it

was

you and me

hopes and

thrills

and a few

disappointments

just to give it all

color

Untangled

it was

hard

but it's

easy

now

because it's all

settled

it's sentences

written——

you have

yours

and I have my

own

and maybe

there can

even be

a place or

two

where they might

overlap

and even if they

don't

that's okay

it's okay

it's simple

Untangled

it

was

there are no more

complications

or knots

or tangles

in a past tense

it's the calm

in a

heart

just before

it opens

again.

Reviews

If you enjoyed *Tangles,* I hope you will consider giving the book a shout-out. Reviews, Tweets, blog posts, etc. are always helpful, and are always appreciated. Recommending a book in-person to your reading friends is also a great way to support your favorite author or a book you love. Word-of-mouth (either online or in real life) still remains the most powerful way to help books find their readership.

Thank you!

Holly Schindler writes for readers of all ages, both the young in years and young at heart. Her works are award-winning and critically acclaimed. She holds a master's degree in English (creative emphasis), and has taught writing courses at the collegiate level. Schindler has also mentored extensively: honing students' creative and scholastic writing, and providing developmental edits to both published and unpublished writers for novels in a variety of genres. A firm believer that reading is as creative an activity as writing, she has worked one-on-one with students in grades K-12 to improve overall literacy skills.

Schindler has been writing poetry since her elementary school days, and writing songs since a member of the Ozark Mountain Daredevils taught her both basic guitar playing and songwriting skills. The influence of music and songwriting is especially evident in *Tangles.*

Schindler enjoys interacting with readers. You can get in touch, check out all the latest releases, or sign up for her newsletter(s) at her author site:

HollySchindler.com

S